WHO'S WHO OF PRO SPORTS

WHO'S WHO OF
PRO
BASEBALL

A GUIDE TO THE GAME'S GREATEST PLAYERS

by Matt Chandler

CAPSTONE PRESS
a capstone imprint

Sports Illustrated Kids Who's Who of Pro Sports are published by Capstone Press,
1710 Roe Crest Drive, North Mankato, Minnesota 56003
www.capstonepub.com

Library of Congress Cataloging-in-Publication Data
Chandler, Matt.
 Who's who of pro baseball : a guide to the game's greatest players / by Matt Chandler.
    pages cm. -- (Sports Illustrated Kids. Who's Who of Pro Sports)
 Includes bibliographical references and index.
 Summary: "Introduces readers to the most dynamic pro baseball stars of today and yesterday, including
notable statistics and records"-- Provided by publisher.
 ISBN 978-1-4914-0892-6 (library binding)
 ISBN 978-1-4914-7610-9 (eBook PDF)
1. Baseball players--Rating of v Juvenile literature.. 2. Baseball players--Biography--Juvenile literature. I.
Title.
 GV865.A1C396 2016
 796.357092'2--dc23
[B]
                              2015002805

Editorial Credits
Nate LeBoutillier, editor; Kyle Grenz, designer; Eric Gohl, media researcher

Photo Credits
Getty Images: Diamond Images, 20, Doug Pensinger, 9; Library of Congress: cover (right), 19 (top), 22
(left), 23 (top), 28; Newscom: Everett Collection, 27, MCT/Rodger Mallison, 17; Shutterstock: Patricia
Hofmeester, 22 (right); Sports Illustrated: Al Tielemans, 16, Damian Strohmeyer, 5, 25, 26, David E. Klutho,
15, Hy Peskin, 19 (bottom), 21, John Biever, 11, John D. Hanlon, 24, John G. Zimmerman, 23 (bottom), John
W. McDonough, cover (middle), 7, Manny Millan, 10, Mark Kauffman, cover (left), Robert Beck, 4, 13, 14,
Simon Bruty, 12

Design Elements: Shutterstock

Printed in the United States of America in North Mankato, Minnesota.
042015   008823CGF15

TABLE OF CONTENTS

DIAMONDS
ON THE DIAMOND

Baseball is a game of power, speed, and precision. Power hitters like David Ortiz launch majestic home runs with booming bats. Speedsters like Andrew McCutchen burn up the basepaths by stealing bases or legging out triples. Pitchers like Clayton Kershaw blow fiery fastballs past defenseless hitters—when they're not fooling them with mind-bending curveballs. Pro baseball's rich history dates back to the late 1800s and is filled with superstars. Who makes your list of the greatest players to ever play the game? They may very well grace the pages of this "Who's Who" guide to pro baseball's greatest players.

DAVID **ORTIZ**

5

GREATS

Modern-Day MVPs

Check out this list of Most Valuable Players (MVPs) from each of the past 15 major league seasons:

Year:	American League (AL):	National League (NL):
2000	Jason **Giambi**, 1B Oakland Athletics	Jeff **Kent**, 2B San Francisco Giants
2001	Ichiro **Suzuki**, RF Seattle Mariners	Barry **Bonds**, LF San Francisco Giants
2002	Miguel **Tejada**, SS Oakland Athletics	Barry **Bonds**, LF San Francisco Giants
2003	Alex **Rodriguez**, SS Texas Rangers	Barry **Bonds**, LF San Francisco Giants
2004	Vladimir **Guerrero**, LF Anaheim Angels	Barry **Bonds**, LF San Francisco Giants
2005	Alex **Rodriguez**, 3B New York Yankees	Albert **Pujols**, 1B St. Louis Cardinals
2006	Justin **Morneau**, 1B Minnesota Twins	Ryan **Howard**, 1B Philadelphia Phillies
2007	Alex **Rodriguez**, 3B New York Yankees	Jimmy **Rollins**, SS Philadelphia Phillies
2008	Dustin **Pedroia**, 2B Boston Red Sox	Albert **Pujols**, 1B St. Louis Cardinals
2009	Joe **Mauer**, C Minnesota Twins	Albert **Pujols**, 1B St. Louis Cardinals
2010	Josh **Hamilton**, CF Texas Rangers	Joey **Votto**, 1B Cincinnati Reds
2011	Justin **Verlander**, P Detroit Tigers	Ryan **Braun**, RF Milwaukee Brewers
2012	Miguel **Cabrera**, 3B Detroit Tigers	Buster **Posey**, C San Francisco Giants
2013	Miguel **Cabrera**, 3B Detroit Tigers	Andrew **McCutchen**, CF Pittsburgh Pirates
2014	Mike **Trout**, CF Los Angeles Angels	Clayton **Kershaw**, P Los Angeles Dodgers

Buster Posey led the NL in batting with a .336 average in his 2012 MVP season. It marked the first time in 70 years that a catcher won an NL batting title.

Buster Busts Out

San Francisco Giants catcher Buster Posey does more than just handle the game behind the plate. Posey made a splash in the major leagues by capturing NL Rookie of the Year honors in 2010. Posey topped off that season by helping the Giants win the World Series. In 2012 Posey helped the Giants to another World Series title and was named the NL MVP. Posey and the Giants won a third World Series title together in 2014.

BUSTER **POSEY**

Best of the Best
Around the Diamond

Major League Baseball (MLB) holds its All-Star game each year at mid-season. The players selected make up an annual "Who's Who" of baseball. The starting lineups at the 2014 All-Star game featured shining stars from top to bottom. Did your favorite player make the list?

NL All-Stars

No.	Name	Pos.
22	Andrew **McCutchen**	CF
66	Yasiel **Puig**	RF
2	Troy **Tulowitzki**	SS
44	Paul **Goldschmidt**	1B
27	Giancarlo **Stanton**	DH
16	Aramis **Ramirez**	3B
26	Chase **Utley**	2B
20	Jonathan **Lucroy**	C
27	Carlos **Gomez**	LF
50	Adam **Wainwright**	P
Mgr.	Mike **Matheny**	(STL)

AL All-Stars

No.	Name	Pos.
2	Derek **Jeter**	SS
27	Mike **Trout**	LF
22	Robinson **Cano**	2B
24	Miguel **Cabrera**	1B
19	Jose **Bautista**	RF
23	Nelson **Cruz**	DH
10	Adam **Jones**	CF
20	Josh **Donaldson**	3B
13	Salvador **Perez**	C
34	Felix **Hernandez**	P
Mgr.	John **Farrell**	(BOS)

REMARKABLE RECORDS Yankees reliever Mariano Rivera won the 1999 World Series MVP and the 2013 All-Star game MVP. He is the only pitcher to ever win MVP of both events.

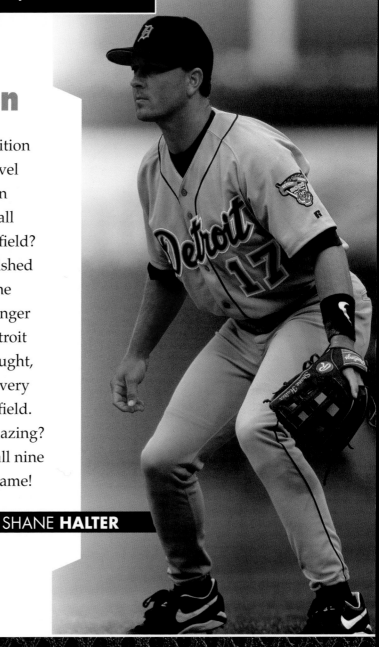

Ultimate Utility Men

To master one position at the major league level is incredibly hard. Can you imagine playing all nine positions on the field? Two players accomplished this amazing feat in the 2000 season. Texas Ranger Scott Sheldon and Detroit Tiger Shane Halter caught, pitched, and played every other position on the field. What's even more amazing? Each player covered all nine positions in a single game!

SHANE **HALTER**

Gods With Gloves

Ozzie Smith was such a great shortstop that he earned the nickname "Wizard" for his glovework. Troy Tulowitzki of the Colorado Rockies and Jimmy Rollins of the Philadelphia Phillies are today's most magical infielders. From 2007 to 2014, either Tulowitzki or Rollins led the NL in fielding percentage.

STAT-TASTIC

Ozzie Smith led the NL in fielding percentage eight times in his 19-year career.

OZZIE **SMITH**

In 2011 Tulowitzki had a career-best .991 fielding percentage. That means that in 140 games at shortstop, "Tulo" had 684 balls hit at him and made only 6 errors!

Pitching In On Defense

Most pitchers rely on their defense to make big plays. Pitcher Mark Buehrle makes plenty of big plays from his spot on the mound. Buehrle works his glove magic by snagging a lot of batted balls to get hitters out. In four separate seasons he has gone the entire year without committing a single error.

From 2009–2011, the hefty lefty collected three straight Gold Glove awards as a member of the Chicago White Sox. Buehrle joined the Miami Marlins in 2012 and captured his fourth Gold Glove award.

MARK **BUEHRLE**

REMARKABLE RECORDS

Relief pitcher Adam Ziegler began his career by tossing a record 39 consecutive scoreless innings from May 31 to August 14, 2008. His effort broke the previous record of 25 innings, set by George McQuillan of the Philadelphia Phillies in 1907.

11

The Pitch That Dances

Many hitters would rather face a flaming fastball than a knuckleball. Fastballs are straight while knuckleballs can dance, dart, and dive suddenly as they float across home plate. Toronto Blue Jays pitcher R.A. Dickey is a master of the knuckler.

R.A. **DICKEY**

In 2014 Dickey was the only starting pitcher in the majors to rely on the knuckleball as his main pitch. Dickey led the NL in starts for three straight seasons from 2012 to 2014. In 2012 Dickey led his league with a 20–6 record and 230 strikeouts to capture the NL Cy Young Award.

REMARKABLE RECORDS

The Los Angeles Angels won 100 games in 2008. Closer Francisco Rodriguez set a major league record by saving 62 of them.

Off the Bench

Pinch-hitting is hard. Imagine being asked to come to bat when the game is on the line and you've been sitting on the bench for hours. Lenny Harris thrived on the pressure. Harris was a utility infielder for eight major league teams from 1988–2005 and holds the career record for most pinch-hits with 212. His ability to deliver in the clutch turned what could have been a short career into 18 seasons in the majors.

STAT-TASTIC

Three hitters have hit homeruns from both sides of the plate in the same inning. Kendrys Morales was the last to do it in 2012 with the Los Angeles Angels.

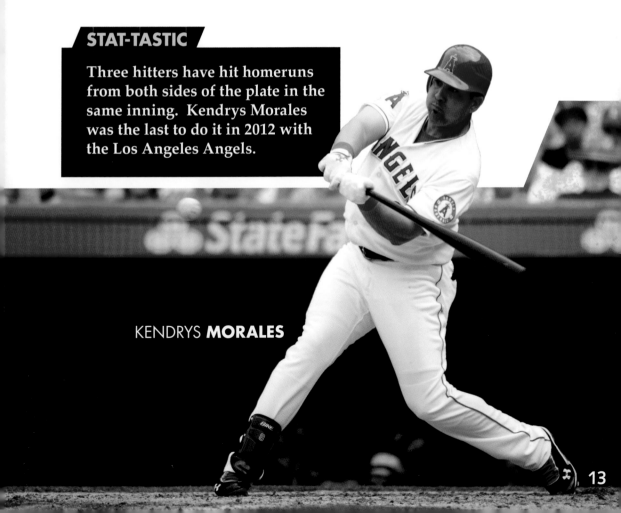

KENDRYS **MORALES**

Pitching to Perfection

To pitch nine innings and take down 27 batters straight without allowing a hit or a baserunner is a nearly impossible task. That's why it's called a perfect game. But that is exactly what Seattle Mariners pitcher Felix Hernandez pitched on August 15, 2012.

Hernandez took just 113 pitches to blank the Tampa Bay Rays and add his name to the history books. Only 23 pitchers in major league history have thrown a perfect game. "King Felix" tossed his at age 26.

FELIX **HERNANDEZ**

STAT-TASTIC

In 135 years of MLB history, there have been just 23 perfect games. In 2012 there were three when Philip Humber, Matt Cain, and Felix Hernandez all reached perfection.

Series Slammer

David Ortiz is one of the best clutch hitters in baseball. He proved it in the 2013 World Series. Ortiz earned the World Series MVP trophy with amazing numbers.

Big Papi reached base 19 times in 25 Series plate appearances, smacked two home runs, and generally carried the Red Sox on his broad shoulders. He dominated Cardinals pitchers so completely that in Game 6, they purposely walked him four times.

REMARKABLE RECORDS

Angel Macias of Mexico threw a perfect game in the championship of the 1957 Little League World Series. It has been the only perfect game pitched in Little League World Series history.

DAVID **ORTIZ**

Clutch to the End

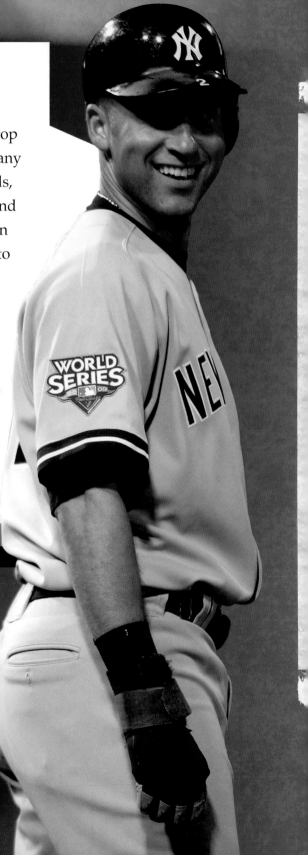

Former New York Yankees shortstop Derek Jeter was never spectacular in any one area. But his solid all-around skills, reliability, and grasp of the play at hand helped him to make the big play when the game was on the line. His ability to deliver when it counted most earned him his nickname, Captain Clutch.

Even at 40 years old, Jeter continued to live up to his nickname. In his final career at-bat at Yankee Stadium in 2014, Captain Clutch drove in the winning run. His walk-off single beat the Baltimore Orioles.

DEREK **JETER**

REMARKABLE RECORDS

Derek Jeter is the only player in major league history to win MVP of the All-Star game and the World Series in the same season. Jeter pulled off the feat in 2000.

Chewy Superstition

Like many baseball players, Cleveland Indians infielder Elliott Johnson has a superstition. Before every at-bat, he chews a piece of watermelon gum. He had a good game once while chewing the gum, and now he won't stop. But Johnson takes his goofy habit even further. Watermelon gum is for hitting. When he takes the field, Johnson switches to grape.

ELLIOTT **JOHNSON**

17

Chapter 2

AGED GREATS

Knocking on the Door

Baseball's greatest players are inducted into the Baseball Hall of Fame in Cooperstown, New York. But what about the superstars who never made the Hall? Here are ten greats you won't find in Cooperstown:

Ross **Barnes**	Infielder who starred for Boston Red Stockings led his league in batting in 1872, 1873, 1876, and batted over .400 in four different seasons.
Larry **Doyle**	Steady second baseman helped his New York Giants to three straight World Series appearances in 1911, 1912, and 1913. He also won 1912 NL MVP.
Dick **Allen**	Corner infield-playing slugger won AL MVP in 1972 and was the middle of three brothers who all made it to the majors.
"Bad" Bill **Dahlen**	The most overlooked of 19th century ball players stole 548 bases and retired in 1912 as baseball's leader in games played with 2,443.
Gil **Hodges**	Only Duke Snider hit more homers in the 1950s than eight-time All-Star Hodges, a longtime Brooklyn Dodger.
Jack **Morris**	Black Jack won 1991 World Series MVP as a Minnesota Twin after pitching a ten-inning shut-out in Game 7. Also pitched for champs in Detroit (1984) and Toronto (1992 and 1993).
Tommy **John**	Crafty left-handed sinkerball pitcher won 288 games with 2,245 strikeouts in 26-season career.
Tony **Mullane**	Irish-born pitcher who played from 1881–1894 never wore a glove and pitched with either hand on the way to 284 wins and 468 complete games.
Minnie **Minoso**	The Cuban Comet broke into the major leagues with the Cleveland Indians in 1949 and starred with the Chicago White Sox. He made the All-Star team seven times.
Jim **McCormick**	First native-born Scottish player in major-league history racked up 265 wins as a pitcher from 1878–1887.

REMARKABLE RECORDS Charlie "Old Hoss" Radbourn won a record 59 games in the 1884 season while pitching for the Providence Grays.

Legendary Leader

Many baseball players have massive egos and wildly different personalities. Managing 25 men through a 162-game season and leading them to victory is a tall order. Connie Mack was a master at managing ballplayers. The Hall of Famer skippered the Pittsburgh Pirates and Philadelphia A's to an all-time best 3,731 wins and a combined five World Series titles.

CONNIE **MACK**

STAT-TASTIC

Today, 20 wins in a season is the mark of success for a pitcher. The legendary Cy Young won 20 or more games in a season 15 times in his career.

MINNIE **MINOSO**

World Series Perfection

For a starting pitcher, there is no bigger thrill than pitching in the World Series. Throwing a perfect game also ranks high on the elite pitcher's wish list. Only one hurler has ever combined these two feats.

On October 8, 1956, Yankees pitcher Don Larsen dominated the Brooklyn Dodgers. Though Dodgers hitters had racked up 1,315 hits during the 1956 season, they were helpless against the man known as Gooneybird. Larsen's perfecto in Game 5 helped the Yankees win the World Series.

YOGI **BERRA** (8) AND DON **LARSEN**
AFTER GAME 5 OF THE 1956 WORLD SERIES

REMARKABLE RECORDS

In 1941 Joe DiMaggio got a hit in 56 consecutive games for the New York Yankees. No hitter since has topped the hitting streak of Joltin' Joe.

Heroes Off the Diamond

Thousands of men were drafted to serve in the United States Armed Forces during World War II (1939–1945). More than 500 major league players served. Legends such as Ted Williams, Stan Musial, and Joe DiMaggio were among those who served during World War II.

Williams is best-known as the last player to hit .400 in a season. But the three years he left the game behind to serve as a Marine lieutenant may be his greatest accomplishment.

TED WILLIAMS

STAT-TASTIC

George Herman "Babe" Ruth led the AL in home runs 12 times. He was also the first player ever to hit 60 homeruns in a season.

Pioneers of the Game

Imagine setting up behind home plate and catching barehanded. That's what players did before the invention of the baseball glove. Here are some of the earliest pioneers of what would become the modern mitt:

Doug **Allison**—The Cincinnati catcher wore a mitt made of buckskin in 1870.

Charles **Waitt**—In 1875 Waitt became the first player to wear a glove full-time.

Joe **Visner**—Visner played from 1885–1891 and was one of the first Native Americans to play professionally. He usually wore no glove.

Bill **Doak**—By 1919, everyone was wearing gloves. But Cardinals pitcher Bill Doak pioneered the creation of the pocket in the glove.

JOE **VISNER**

Longball Legends

There are few things as exciting as watching a batter crush a home run. Take a look at the top homerun hitters of each decade from 1870–1960.

1870	Lip **Pike**	21
1880s	Harry **Stovey**	89
1890s	Hugh **Duffy**	83
1900s	Harry **Davis**	67
1910s	Clifford **Cravath**	116
1920s	Babe **Ruth**	467
1930s	Jimmie **Foxx**	415
1940s	Ted **Williams**	234
1950s	Duke **Snider**	326
1960s	Harmon **Killebrew**	393

STAT-TASTIC

In 1920—and again in 1927—Babe Ruth hit more home runs than every other team in the American League!

REMARKABLE RECORDS

The base runner always has the advantage when stealing a base, unless the runner was challenging Roy Campanella's arm. Over his career, the Dodger catcher threw out a record 57 percent of the base runners who tried to steal.

23

Awesome in Oakland

In the first half of the 1970s, no team was as dominant as the Oakland Athletics. The A's won five straight division titles from 1971–1975. Oakland was led by a trio of future Hall of Famers during its red-hot stretch. Pitchers Rollie Fingers and Catfish Hunter and super-slugging outfielder Reggie Jackson anchored the title teams of the '70s. Winning three consecutive World Series cemented the A's as one of baseball's all-time greatest dynasties.

CATFISH **HUNTER**

STAT-TASTIC

The St. Louis Cardinals won 19 NL pennants between 1926 and 2013. The Cardinals went on to claim the World Series trophy 11 times.

The Bronx Bombers

The New York Yankees are Major League Baseball's most decorated team. The Yankees' success continues today. Since 2000 the boys in pinstripes won the AL East division 10 times. Four of those seasons produced more than 100 wins, and the Yanks played in four Fall Classics. The Yankees' most recent dynasty will be remembered for superstars Derek Jeter and Mariano Rivera. But it took hundreds of solid players to build a decade-plus of dominance in New York.

NEW YORK **YANKEES**
2009 WORLD SERIES

The Rivalry That Babe Built

There is no bigger rivalry in baseball than the Boston Red Sox versus the New York Yankees. The rivalry stretches back to 1919 when Red Sox owner Harry Frazee sold Babe Ruth to the Yankees for $100,000. Ruth led the Yankees to four World titles while Boston didn't win a series again for 86 years.

The two teams have locked horns more than 2,000 times, with the Yankees holding the overall edge. New York also has more World Series championships with 27 titles to Boston's 8.

REMARKABLE RECORDS

Stan "The Man" Musial faced pitcher Warren Spahn 383 times in his career. Though Musial thumped 106 hits off of his rival, his .277 batting average against Spahn was well below his .331 career average.

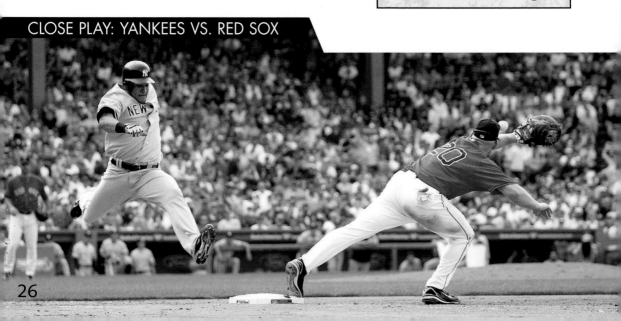

CLOSE PLAY: YANKEES VS. RED SOX

BROTHERS JOE (LEFT) AND PHIL **NIEKRO**

Sibling Rivalry

Do you have a brother or sister? Are you competitive with them? Now imagine if you both played in the major leagues. Knuckleball pitchers Phil and Joe Niekro combined for 539 wins in their careers. But the brothers were fierce competitors. They faced each other nine times with the younger Joe beating Phil in five of nine games. Joe got the best of Phil at the plate as well. In 973 career at-bats, Joe hit only one homerun. Guess who served up the juicy pitch? Yep. Big brother Phil.

STAT-TASTIC

The Giants and Dodgers have faced off more than 2,300 times. Both teams began in New York and the rivalry continued when the franchises moved to California.

Championship Cubs

Today the Chicago Cubs are known as the team with the longest World Series title drought—more than 106 years. But in 1907, the Cubbies put together one of the best seasons ever. Led by two 20-game winners (Orval Overall, 23-7, and Mordecai Brown, 20-6) the Cubs were dominant. They won the NL title by 17 games and swept the Detroit Tigers to win the team's first World Series title.

REMARKABLE **RECORDS**

The Chicago Cubs won a record 116 games in 1906. Amazingly, they went on to lose the World Series to their cross-town rivals, the White Sox.

Giants on the Diamond

Long before they moved to San Francisco, the Giants dominated New York. The 1904 season may have been their greatest ever. The Giants had two 30-game winners, including Joe McGinnity (35–8) and Christy Mathewson (33–12). Their offense was unmatched as well, outscoring their opponents by 270 runs. There was no World Series played in 1904, but any baseball historian will tell you the Giants were the 1904 champs!

WONDERMENTS

Fantastic Records

Last man to hit three homeruns in a single World Series game:

Reggie **Jackson**

Hit by a pitch 287 times in his career:

Hughie **Jennings**

Only pitcher to throw consecutive no-hitters:

Johnny **Vander Meer**

Only pitcher to throw seven career no-hitters:

Nolan **Ryan**

Played 2,632 games in a row without missing a start:

Cal **Ripken** Jr.

Last player to hit over .400 in a season:

Ted **Williams**

Hit two grand slams in the same inning:

Fernando **Tatis**

Elected to 25 All-Star Games:

Hank **Aaron**

Most pinch hits in a career:

Lenny **Harris** (212)

Earned 4,256 career hits:

Pete **Rose**

Best Nicknames of Today

Felix **Hernandez**
" King Felix "

Aroldis **Chapman**
" The Cuban Missile "

Johnny **Damon**
" The Caveman "

Frank **Thomas**
" The Big Hurt "

Derek **Jeter**
" Captain Clutch "

Ryan **Braun**
" The Hebrew Hammer "

Dustin **Pedroia**
" The Laser Show "

Pedro **Alvarez**
" The Big Bull "

Shane **Victorino**
" The Flyin' Hawaiian "

David **Ortiz**
" Big Papi "

Best Nicknames of Yesteryear

Pete **Rose**
" Charlie Hustle "

Babe **Ruth**
" The Sultan of Swat "

Nolan **Ryan**
" The Ryan Express "

Lou **Gehrig**
" Biscuit Pants "

Willie **Mays**
" The Say Hey Kid "

Rickey **Henderson**
" Man of Steal "

Gabby **Hartnett**
" Old Tomato Face "

Steve **Lyons**
" Psycho "

Lenny **Dykstra**
" Nails "

Randy **Johnson**
" The Big Unit "

Glossary

clutch (KLUTCH)—in sports, occurring at a critical situation in which the outcome of a game or competition is at stake

consecutive (kuhn-SEK-yuh-tiv)—when something happens several times in a row without a break

dominate (DAH-muh-nayt)—to rule; in sports, a team or person dominates if they win significantly more than anyone else

dynasty (DYE-nuh-stee)—a team that wins multiple championships over a period of several years

error (AYR-ur)—when a defensive player makes a mistake while fielding the ball

fielding percentage (FEEL-ding pur-SENT-ij)—a measure that reflects the rate at which a defensive player properly handles a batted or thrown ball

pennant (PEN-uhnt)—in baseball, the prize that is awarded to the champions of the American League and the National League each year

pinch hitter (PINCH HIT-ur)—a substitute batter who has not yet entered the game

rivalry (RYE-val-ree)—a fierce feeling of competition between two teams

superstition (soo-pur-STI-shuhn)—a belief that an action can affect the outcome of a future event

utility player (yoo-TIL-uh-tee PLAY-ur)—a player capable of playing well in any of several positions

walk-off hit (WALK-OFF HIT)—a game-winning hit in the bottom half of the last inning of a game

Read More

Chandler, Matt. *Side-by-Side Baseball Stars: Comparing Pro Baseball's Greatest Players.* North Mankato, Minn.: Capstone Press, 2015.

Hammer, Max. *Superstars of the Boston Red Sox.* Mankato, Minn.: Amicus High Interest, 2015.

LeBoutillier, Nate. *The Ultimate Guide to Pro Baseball Teams.* Mankato, Minn.: Capstone Press, 2011.

Internet Sites

FactHound offers a safe, fun way to find Internet sites related to this book. All of the sites on FactHound have been researched by our staff.

Here's all you do:

Visit *www.facthound.com*

Type in this code: 9781491408926

Check out projects, games and lots more at
www.capstonekids.com

Index